CAMBRIDGE PRIMARY MATHEMATICS

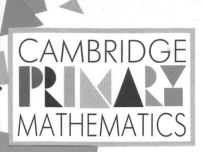

MATHS FOUR
BOOK 2

Roy Edwards
Mary Edwards
Alan Ward

CAMBRIDGE
UNIVERSITY PRESS

Published by the Press Syndicate of the University of Cambridge
The Pitt Building, Trumpington Street, Cambridge CB2 1RP
40 West 20th Street, New York, NY 10011–4211, USA
10 Stamford Road, Oakleigh, Victoria 3166, Australia

First published 1989
Reprinted 1992

Printed in Great Britain at the University Press, Cambridge

British Library cataloguing in publication data
Edwards, Roy
Cambridge primary mathematics,
Module 4
Bk. 2
1. Mathematics – For schools
I. Title   II. Edwards, Mary   III. Ward, Alan
510

ISBN 0-521-35821-3

The authors and publishers would like to thank the many schools
and individuals who have commented on draft material for this
course. In particular, they would like to thank Anita Straker for
her contribution to the suggestions for work with computers,
Norma Anderson, Ronalyn Hargreaves (Hyndburn Ethnic
Minority Support Service) and John Hyland Advisory Teacher
in Tameside, and the staff and pupils of Teversham School.

Photographs are reproduced courtesy of;
front cover ZEFA; p33 Valiant Technology; p75 Paul Hutley.
All other photographs by Reeve Photography, Graham Portlock,
Justin Munro and Nigel Luckhurst.

The mathematical apparatus was kindly supplied by E J Arnold.
Hestaire Hope supplied the primary ruler (p18).

Designed by Chris McLeod

Illustrations by Chris Ryley, Kim Palmer and John Grisenthwaite
Children's illustrations by Amy Quinn, George McLeod and
Lucy Bowden
Diagrams by DP Press

DP

Contents

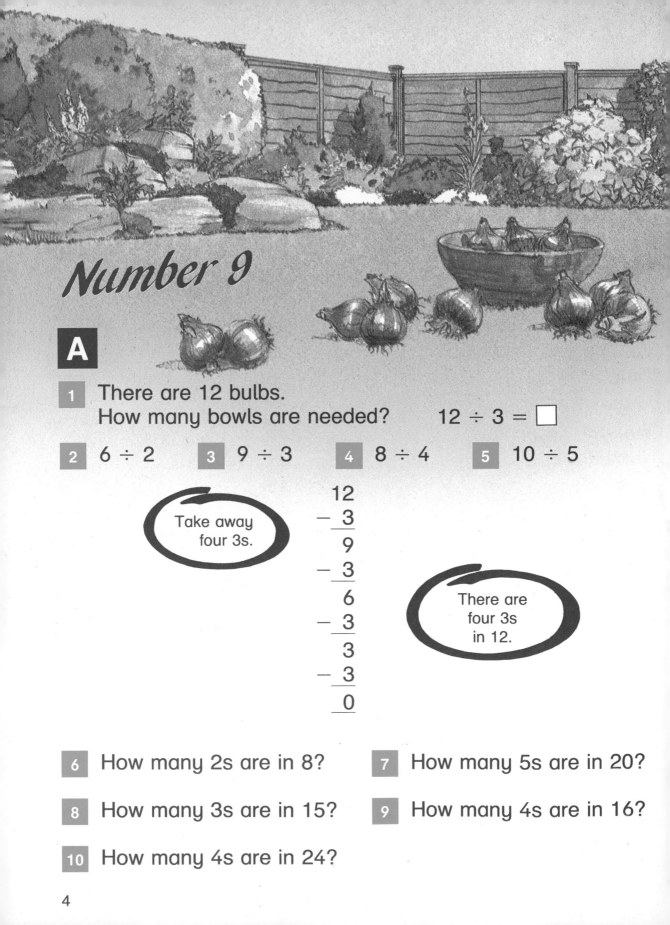

Number 9

A

1 There are 12 bulbs.
How many bowls are needed? $12 \div 3 = \square$

2 $6 \div 2$ 3 $9 \div 3$ 4 $8 \div 4$ 5 $10 \div 5$

Take away
four 3s.

$$
\begin{array}{r}
12 \\
- \ 3 \\
\hline
9 \\
- \ 3 \\
\hline
6 \\
- \ 3 \\
\hline
3 \\
- \ 3 \\
\hline
0 \\
\end{array}
$$

There are
four 3s
in 12.

6 How many 2s are in 8?   7 How many 5s are in 20?

8 How many 3s are in 15?   9 How many 4s are in 16?

10 How many 4s are in 24?

4

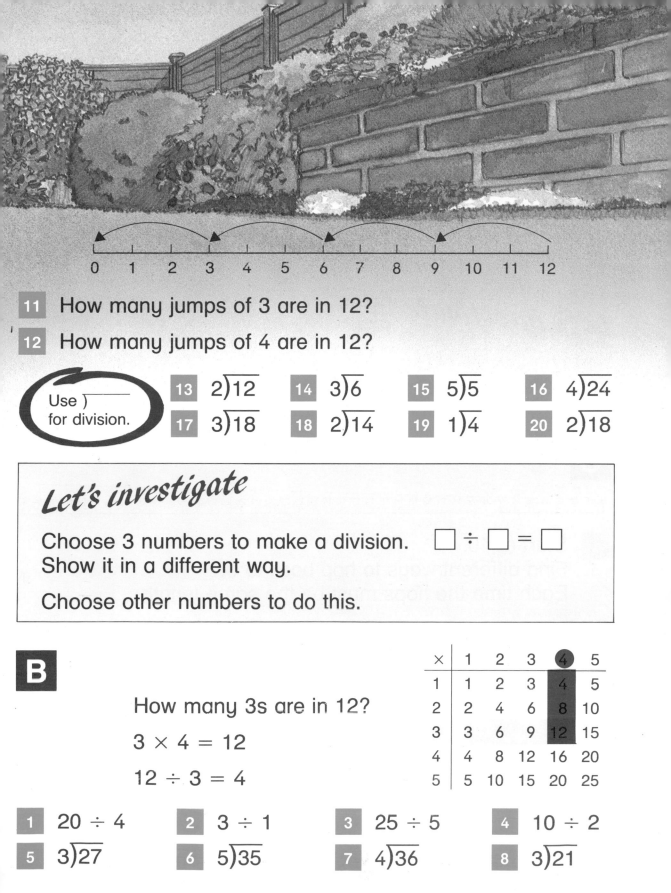

11 How many jumps of 3 are in 12?

12 How many jumps of 4 are in 12?

Use ⟌ for division.

13 2⟌12   **14** 3⟌6   **15** 5⟌5   **16** 4⟌24

17 3⟌18   **18** 2⟌14   **19** 1⟌4   **20** 2⟌18

Let's investigate

Choose 3 numbers to make a division.   □ ÷ □ = □
Show it in a different way.

Choose other numbers to do this.

B

How many 3s are in 12?

$3 \times 4 = 12$

$12 \div 3 = 4$

×	1	2	3	4	5
1	1	2	3	4	5
2	2	4	6	8	10
3	3	6	9	12	15
4	4	8	12	16	20
5	5	10	15	20	25

1 20 ÷ 4   **2** 3 ÷ 1   **3** 25 ÷ 5   **4** 10 ÷ 2

5 3⟌27   **6** 5⟌35   **7** 4⟌36   **8** 3⟌21

5

9 4 plants go into each pot.
How many pots are needed for 16 plants?

10 How many pots are needed for 24 plants?

Let's investigate

You can use 20 bricks.
Draw different walls you could build.
Each row must be the same length.

C

0 1 2 3 4 5 6 7 8 9 10 11 12 13 14 15 16 17 18 19 20 21 22 23 24 25 26 27 28 29 30 31 32 33 34 35 36 37 38 39 40

1 Start at 40.
Find different ways to hop back to 0.
Each time the hops must be the same length.

Let's investigate

Which boxes can the flowers be put in?
Find different ways of putting one bunch in each box.

Data 2

A

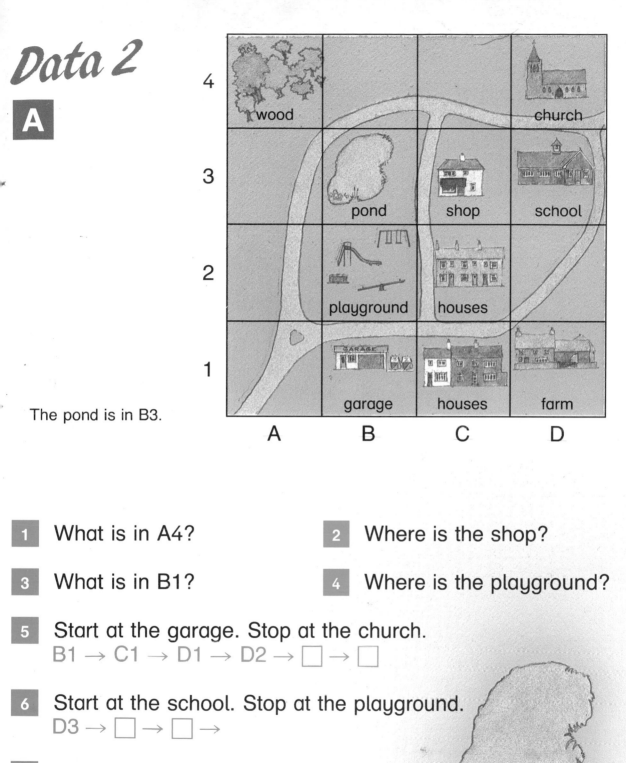

The pond is in B3.

1 What is in A4?

2 Where is the shop?

3 What is in B1?

4 Where is the playground?

5 Start at the garage. Stop at the church.
B1 → C1 → D1 → D2 → ☐ → ☐

6 Start at the school. Stop at the playground.
D3 → ☐ → ☐ →

7 Start at the pond. Stop at the farm.
☐ → ☐ →

Find another way.

Let's investigate

Draw this plan of a playground.

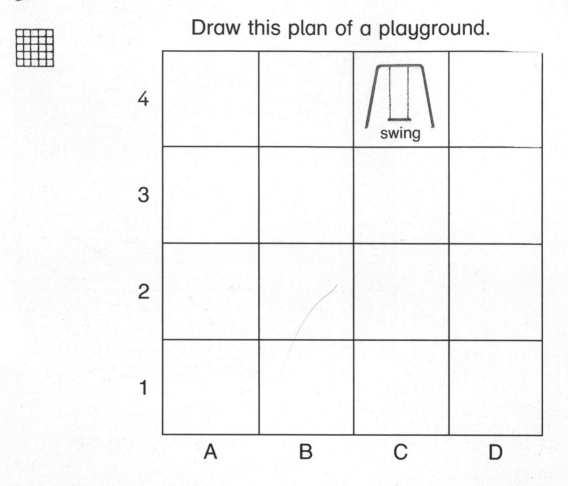

swing

A   B   C   D

Put these in the playground.

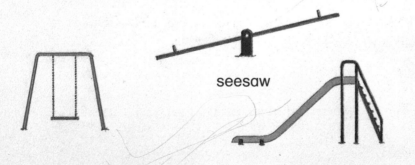

seesaw

swing

slide

climbing frame

Add some more things.
Write their squares.

B

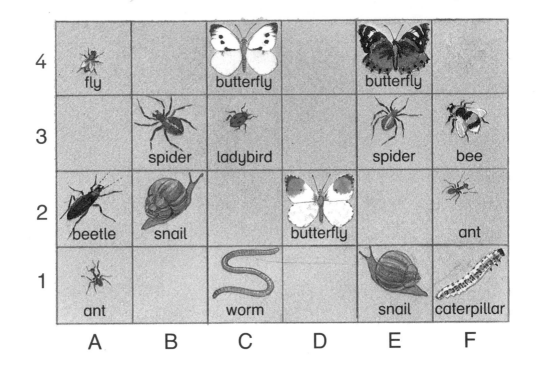

1. Where is the bee? 2. What is in square A2?

3. What is nearest the fly? Write its square.

4. What are nearest the caterpillar? Write their squares.

5. Where are the ants?

6. There are three of one creature. Write their squares.

7. The worm goes to the same square as the bee.
   Write the squares it travels through.

Let's investigate

Here is a word in code.

C3-A1-C1-B3-A2-B2-C2-A3-B1

What is the word?

Write other words in code.

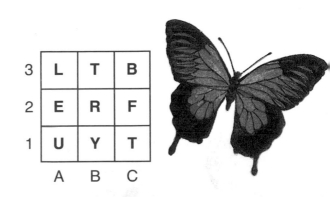

	A	B	C
3	L	T	B
2	E	R	F
1	U	Y	T

farmhouse	B2
barn	C3
stable	E2
tree	E4
field	C4
tractor	D4
dog kennel	C2
geese	A2
pond	A1
hen-house	D2
haystack	B3

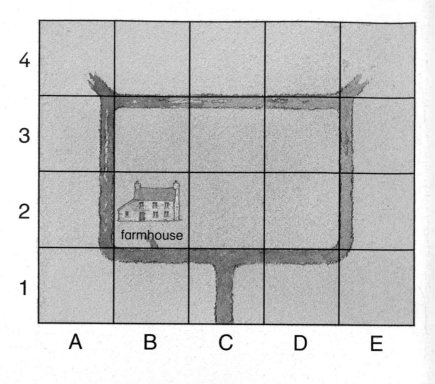

farmhouse

1 Copy the plan of the farm.
Draw or write the things in their right squares.

2 Plan a journey round the farm.
Write the squares and names
of the things you see.

Let's investigate

There are 4 sheep, 4 geese,
4 cows and 4 hens.

Put them in their pens.

There must be one of each animal
in each row **and** in each column.
Write their squares.

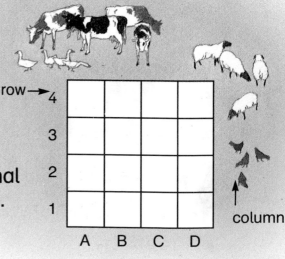

row ➔ 4

3

2

1

column

A B C D

NASREEN DAR STORE
Tel. 314987

How much are these?

1 4 fizzers ☐ p   2 3 twists ☐ p

3 7 chews ☐ p   4 5 pops ☐ p

5 2 twists and 2 pops ☐ p

6 3 fizzers and 2 chews ☐ p

fizzer 3p

twist 5p

chew 2p

pop 4p

7 How many fizzers for 18p?

8 How many pops for 24p?

How much change do I get?

9   I have 10p. I spend 8p. My change is ☐ p.

10 I have 15p. I spend 4p. My change is ☐ p.

11 I have 20p. I spend 16p. My change is ☐ p.

12 I have 12p. I spend 7p. My change is ☐ p.

Work out these bills.

13	p	14	p	15	p
	25		36		32
+	38	+	25	+	36

Chocolate 38p

Digestives 32p

16 Choose two packets of biscuits.
Write the bill.

Wafers 36p

17 How much change from 40p
for each packet of biscuits?

Ginger 25p

Let's investigate

Janet has these coins.
She loses three coins.
How much can she have lost?

B

JAGS NEWSAGENTS
41 TRUMPINGTON ST, CAMBRIDGE 357295

1. How many pencils can you buy for 60p?

2. How many rubbers do you get for 90p?

3. How many pens do you get for 60p?

   pencil 20p

4. 1 pen, 1 pencil and 1 rubber cost ☐ p.
   How much change from 80p?

   rubber 30p

5. 1 rubber and 1 notebook cost ☐ p.
   How much change from 75p?

   pen 15p

6. 2 pens and 1 notebook cost ☐ p.
   How much change from 60p?

   notebook 18p

Let's investigate

Find some ways of making up 80p.

C Draw the smallest number of stamps needed for each parcel.

1 2 3 4

86p 56p 79p 93p

1p
2p
3p
4p
5p
10p
14p
19p
20p
22p
23p
27p
28p
32p
50p

Let's investigate

Design a 50p page of stamps.
You must be able to send
1st class and 2nd class letters.

Design some more pages.
Each page must add up to 50p.

Number 10

A ✂

1

Use three paper circles.
Fold and make halves.

How many halves are there?

2

Use two circles.
Make quarters.

How many are there?

3

Use three circles.
Make 3 halves and
6 quarters.

4 Make a fraction wall.
Use three strips of paper.

	1	1	1
		$\frac{1}{2}$ $\frac{1}{2}$	$\frac{1}{2}$ $\frac{1}{2}$
			$\frac{1}{4}$ $\frac{1}{4}$ $\frac{1}{4}$ $\frac{1}{4}$

Stick the wall in your book. ✏

5 $\frac{2}{2} = \boxed{}$

6 $\frac{4}{4} = \boxed{}$

7 $\frac{2}{4} = \frac{\boxed{}}{\boxed{}}$

Let's investigate

Draw this flag.

Colour 2 quarters red.

Colour 2 quarters green.

Draw another flag.

Colour $\frac{1}{2}$ blue.

Colour $\frac{1}{4}$ black.

Colour $\frac{1}{4}$ yellow.

B

1   Use three paper squares.

Divide each square into quarters in different ways.

Colour half of each square.

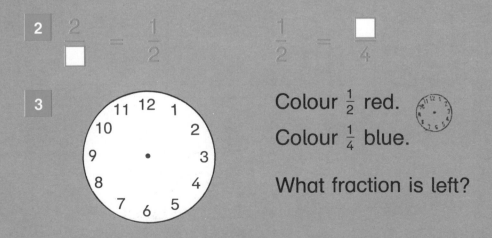

2   $\frac{2}{\square} = \frac{1}{2}$ $\frac{1}{2} = \frac{\square}{4}$

3   Colour $\frac{1}{2}$ red.

Colour $\frac{1}{4}$ blue.

What fraction is left?

Let's investigate

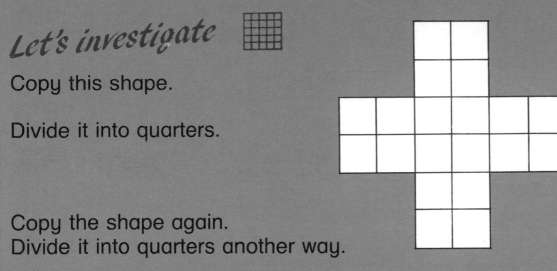

Copy this shape.

Divide it into quarters.

Copy the shape again.
Divide it into quarters another way.

How many different ways can you find?

C   Use two paper triangles like these.

1   Fold one into halves.

2   Fold the other into quarters.

Let's investigate

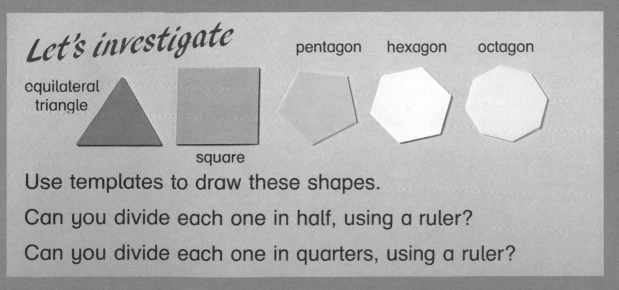

pentagon   hexagon   octagon

equilateral
triangle

square

Use templates to draw these shapes.

Can you divide each one in half, using a ruler?

Can you divide each one in quarters, using a ruler?

Length 2

cm means centimetres.

A ruler measures in centimetres.

1 How long is your ruler? ☐ cm

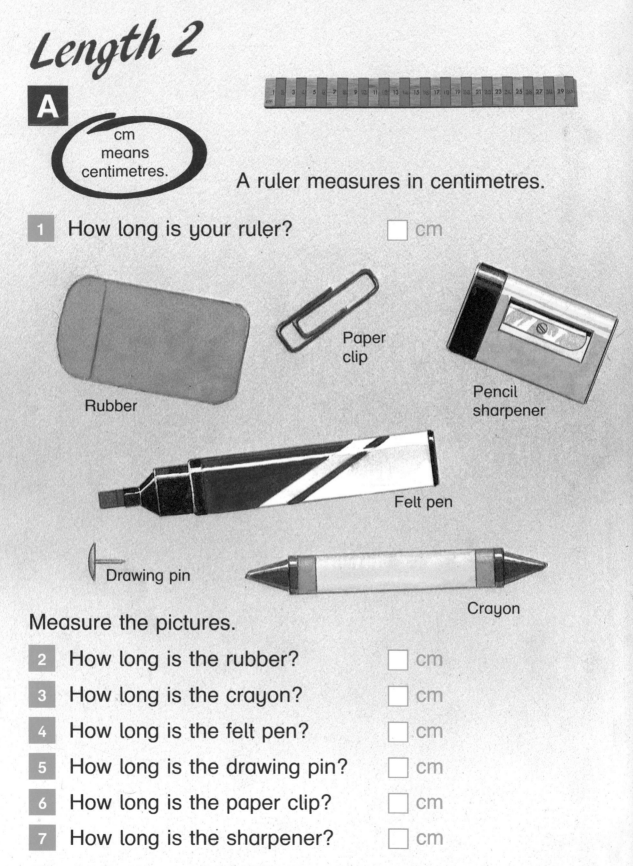

Rubber

Paper clip

Pencil sharpener

Felt pen

Drawing pin

Crayon

Measure the pictures.

2 How long is the rubber? ☐ cm

3 How long is the crayon? ☐ cm

4 How long is the felt pen? ☐ cm

5 How long is the drawing pin? ☐ cm

6 How long is the paper clip? ☐ cm

7 How long is the sharpener? ☐ cm

8 Use your ruler.
Draw a line 5 cm long.

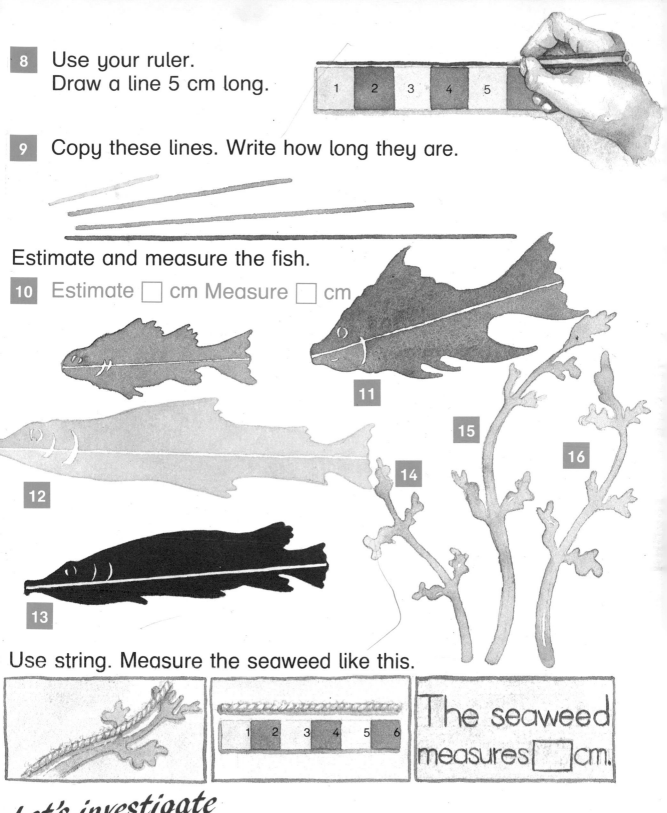

9 Copy these lines. Write how long they are.

Estimate and measure the fish.

10 Estimate ☐ cm Measure ☐ cm

11

12

13

14

15

16

Use string. Measure the seaweed like this.

The seaweed measures ☐ cm.

Let's investigate

Choose one of the fish. Draw it twice as big.

B Use string. Measure the pipe-cleaners.

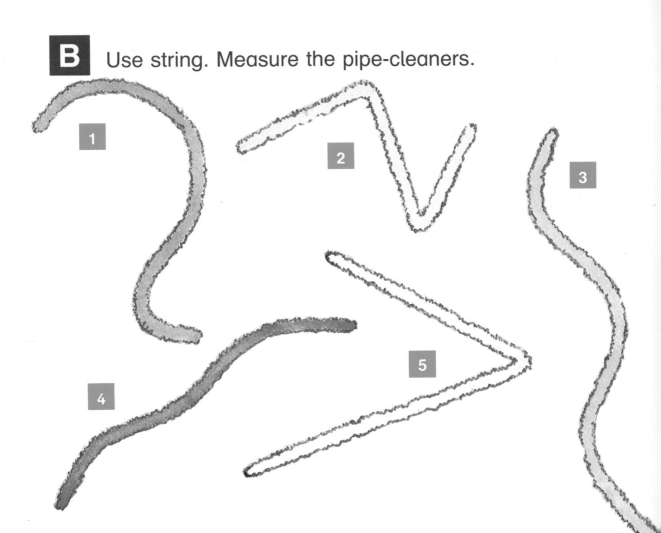

6 Make a mini-ruler.

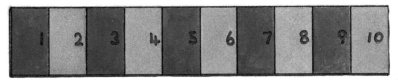

Find things about the same length.
Make a list.

7 Make these rulers.
5 cm   15 cm   20 cm

Make a list of things that
are about these lengths.

8 Stretch out your hand.
Draw round it.
Estimate your span. My estimate is ☐ cm.
Measure your span. My span is ☐ cm.

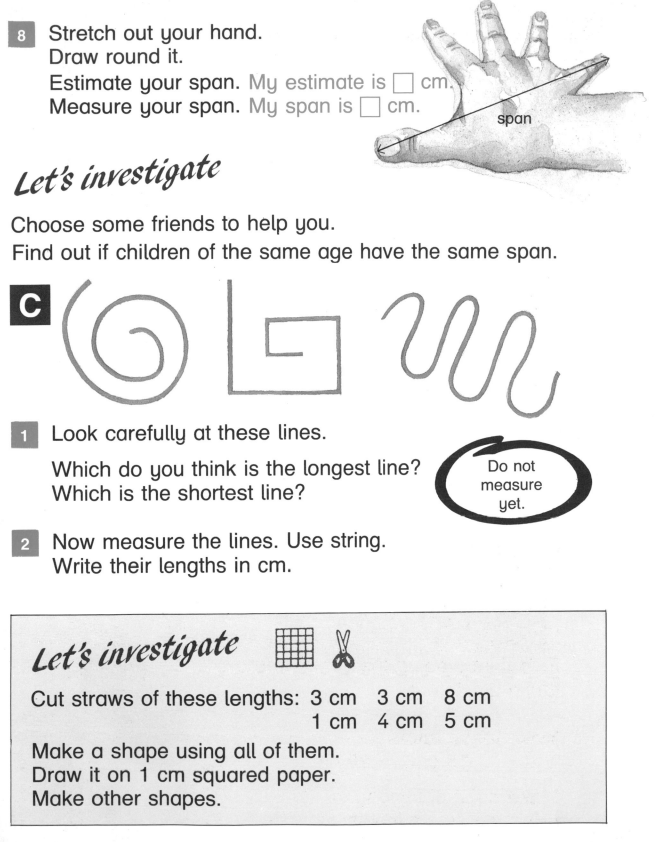

span

Let's investigate

Choose some friends to help you.
Find out if children of the same age have the same span.

C

1 Look carefully at these lines.

Which do you think is the longest line?
Which is the shortest line?

Do not
measure
yet.

2 Now measure the lines. Use string.
Write their lengths in cm.

Let's investigate

Cut straws of these lengths: 3 cm   3 cm   8 cm
                              1 cm   4 cm   5 cm

Make a shape using all of them.
Draw it on 1 cm squared paper.
Make other shapes.

A

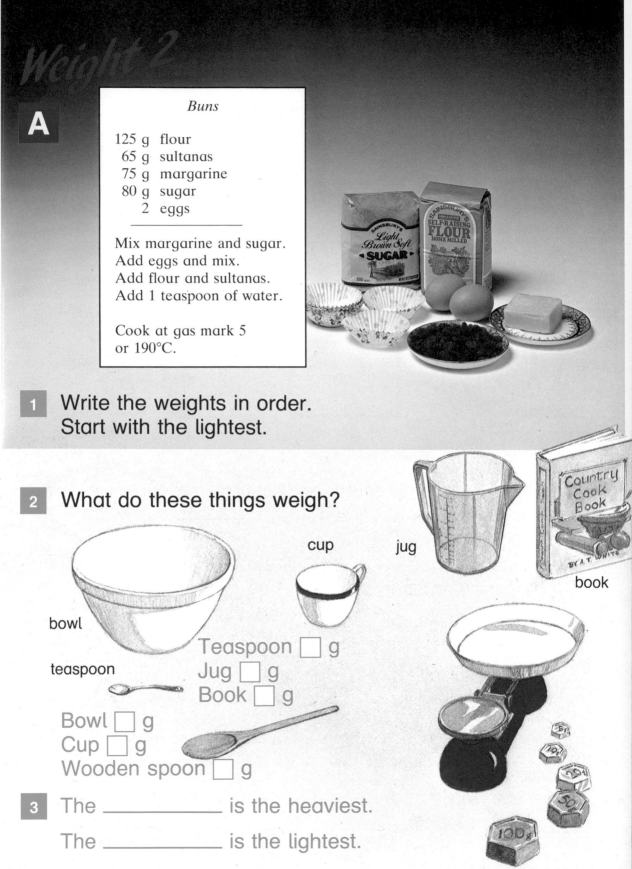

Buns

125 g flour
 65 g sultanas
 75 g margarine
 80 g sugar
  2 eggs
_____

Mix margarine and sugar.
Add eggs and mix.
Add flour and sultanas.
Add 1 teaspoon of water.

Cook at gas mark 5
or 190°C.

1 Write the weights in order.
Start with the lightest.

2 What do these things weigh?

cup   jug

book

bowl

teaspoon

Teaspoon ☐ g
Jug ☐ g
Book ☐ g

Bowl ☐ g
Cup ☐ g
Wooden spoon ☐ g

3 The _____ is the heaviest.

The _____ is the lightest.

4 Find things that weigh about 200 g.
Make a list.

5 Find things that weigh about 500 g.
Make a list.

Let's investigate

Find ways to balance 200 g.

Use two weights. What are they?
Use three weights. What are they?
Use four weights. What are they?

What other sets of weights can you use?

B

75 g
margarine

125 g
flour

80 g
sugar

Laura is making buns.
What weights does she need?

1 Sugar ☐ g + ☐ g + ☐ g

2 Margarine **3** Flour **4** Sultanas

65 g
sultanas

23

5 Make weights of 50 g and 200 g.
Use these things.
Label your weights.

Let's investigate

Use your 50 g and 200 g weights.
Find a way to make a 150 g lump of plasticine.

Can you find a way to make a 100 g lump?

Find how to make other weights of plasticine.

C What do these lunches weigh?

1 **2** **3**

Lunch weights	
2 Sandwiches	90 g
Crisps	25 g
Drink	350 g
Apple	150 g
Banana	125 g
Orange	200 g
Cake	50 g
Chocolate	25 g

4 Which lunch is heaviest?

Let's investigate

Use the chart above.
Make different lunch packs that weigh the same.
You may use some things more than once.

Volume and Capacity 2

1 Pour water from a litre bottle into a cup.

   1 litre fills ☐ cups.

2 Pour cups of water into a litre measure.

   ☐ cups fill the litre measure.

3 ☐ cups fill a $\frac{1}{2}$ litre measure.

4 Think of ways of using water.
   Write down as many as you can.

5 Does a paint pot hold more or less than 1 litre?

6 Which hold less than 1 litre?

Which hold more than 1 litre?

Which hold less than $\frac{1}{2}$ litre?

mug

cup

jug

teapot

kettle

Let's investigate

When do you use more than 1 litre of water at home?

Draw or write your answers.

B How many of each fill the litre measure?

Estimate, then measure.

1 Pot   estimate ☐
           measure ☐

2 Mug   estimate ☐
           measure ☐

3 Jug   estimate ☐
           measure ☐

4 How many litres fill the bucket?

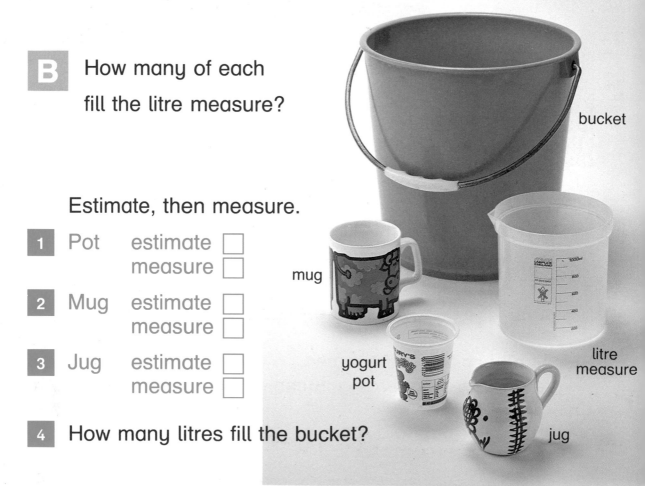

bucket

mug

yogurt pot

litre measure

jug

5 The water bottle holds 4 litres.
The jug holds $\frac{1}{2}$ litre.

How many jugs can be filled?

Let's investigate

Find some containers which hold 1 litre.
They must be different shapes.

Write a sentence about the shape of a litre.

C Let's investigate

A mug holds about $\frac{1}{4}$ litre.

How much do you drink with your meals?

How much do you drink in one day?

Estimate how many litres you drink in one week.

How many litres do your friends drink?

27

Time 2

A Write the times.

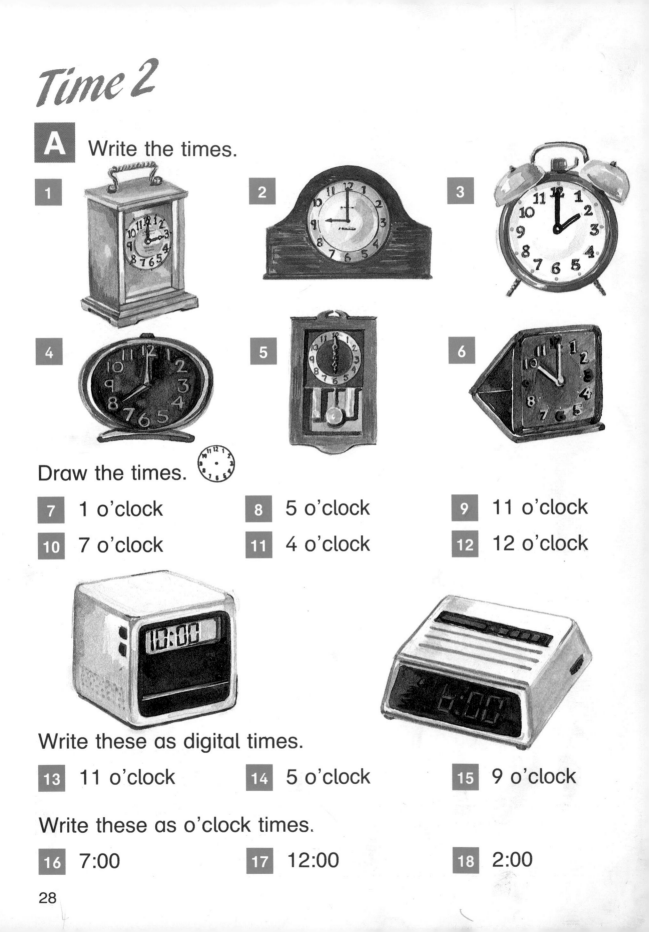

1

2

3

4

5

6

Draw the times.

7 1 o'clock

8 5 o'clock

9 11 o'clock

10 7 o'clock

11 4 o'clock

12 12 o'clock

Write these as digital times.

13 11 o'clock

14 5 o'clock

15 9 o'clock

Write these as o'clock times.

16 7:00

17 12:00

18 2:00

28

Write the times.

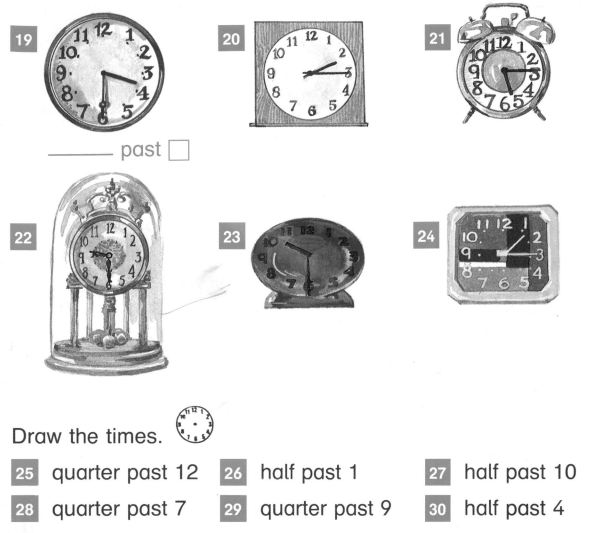

19 _____ past ☐

20

21

22

23

24

Draw the times.

| 25 | quarter past 12 | 26 | half past 1 | 27 | half past 10 |
| 28 | quarter past 7 | 29 | quarter past 9 | 30 | half past 4 |

Let's investigate

Choose four times in the day.
Draw pictures for the times.
Show what you do at the times.

B

Draw times one hour before.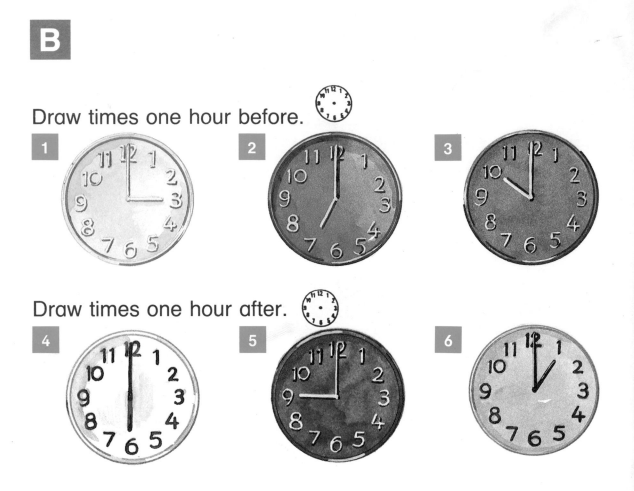

| 1 | 2 | 3 |

Draw times one hour after.

| 4 | 5 | 6 |

7 Write the times in order.

Stamp clock faces in your book.

Colour $\frac{1}{2}$ an hour on each clock in a different way.

C Draw the times.

1

2 hours before

2

1 hour after

3

$\frac{1}{2}$ hour before

4

$\frac{1}{4}$ hour before

5

$\frac{1}{4}$ hour after

6

3 hours after

Let's investigate

The clock shows $\frac{1}{4}$ hour jumps.

How many ways can you show $\frac{1}{4}$ hour jumps?

31

Angles 2

A

house

tractor

pond

barn

1 Look at the house. Make a full turn left. See _____ .

2 Look at the barn. Make a full turn right. See _____ .

3 Look at the house. Make a $\frac{1}{2}$ turn right. See _____ .

4 Look at the tractor. Make a $\frac{1}{2}$ turn left. See _____ .

5 Look at the house. Make a $\frac{1}{4}$ turn left. See _____ .

6 Look at the barn. Make a $\frac{1}{4}$ turn right. See _____ .

7 Look at the pond. Make a $\frac{1}{4}$ turn left. See _____ .

8 Look at the tractor. Make a $\frac{1}{4}$ turn right. See _____ .

9 Look at the house. Make a $\frac{1}{2}$ turn left. See _____ .

10 Look at the barn. Make a $\frac{1}{4}$ turn left. See _____ .

Let's investigate

Make up some moves for a friend, like this.

Face the barn.
Make a $\frac{1}{2}$ turn right and a $\frac{1}{4}$ turn left.
What do you see?

B

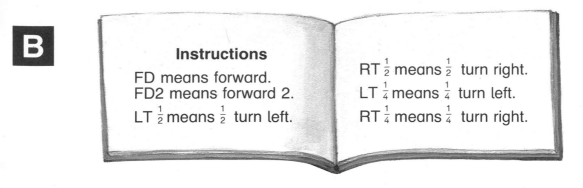

Instructions

FD means forward.
FD2 means forward 2.
LT $\frac{1}{2}$ means $\frac{1}{2}$ turn left.

RT $\frac{1}{2}$ means $\frac{1}{2}$ turn right.
LT $\frac{1}{4}$ means $\frac{1}{4}$ turn left.
RT $\frac{1}{4}$ means $\frac{1}{4}$ turn right.

These instructions move the turtle
from start to   A   to   B   to stop.

Start FD2 → RT $\frac{1}{4}$ → FD3 →

LT $\frac{1}{4}$ → FD1 Stop

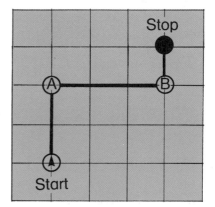

Write instructions for these.

1

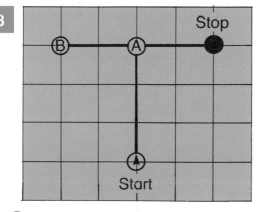

☐ → ☐ → ☐

2

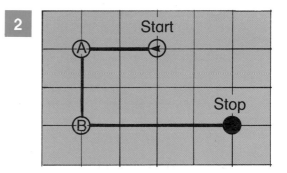

3

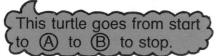
This turtle goes from start
to Ⓐ to Ⓑ to stop.

33

Let's investigate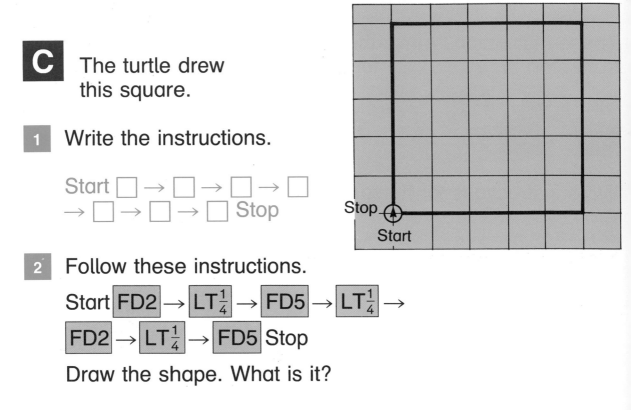

Draw turtle paths of your own.
Show where the turtle starts and stops.

Write instructions for the paths.

C The turtle drew
this square.

1 Write the instructions.

Start ☐ → ☐ → ☐ → ☐
→ ☐ → ☐ → ☐ Stop

Stop

Start

2 Follow these instructions.

Start FD2 → LT$\frac{1}{4}$ → FD5 → LT$\frac{1}{4}$ →
FD2 → LT$\frac{1}{4}$ → FD5 Stop

Draw the shape. What is it?

Let's investigate

Use squared paper.

Keep to the lines.

Draw a six-sided shape.

Write different ways for the turtle to draw the same
six-sided shape.

Number 11

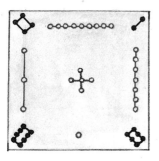

This square is from China.
It is very old.

1 Now it looks like this.
Copy it and finish it.

2 Add each line.
What do you get?
This is the magic number.

4	9	2
		7

Copy these squares. Finish them.

3

3		7
10	6	
5		9

Magic number 18

4

	6	
4		12
9	10	5

Magic number 24

These are
magic squares

Find the patterns. Write the numbers.

5 3 13 23 ⚬ ⚬ ⚬ 63

6 9 19 ⚬ ⚬ ⚬ ⚬ 69

7 38 48 ⚬ ⚬ ⚬ ⚬ 98

8 15 25 ⚬ ⚬ ⚬ ⚬ 75

Look for number patterns.

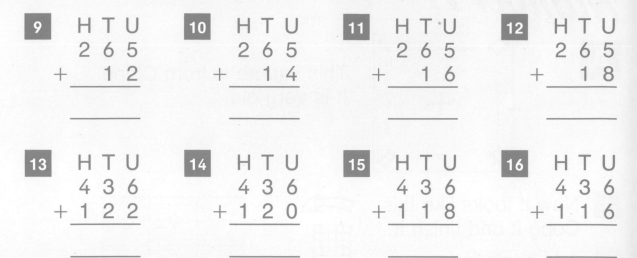

9 H T U
  2 6 5
+   1 2
―――

10 H T U
  2 6 5
+   1 4
―――

11 H T U
  2 6 5
+   1 6
―――

12 H T U
  2 6 5
+   1 8
―――

13 H T U
  4 3 6
+ 1 2 2
―――

14 H T U
  4 3 6
+ 1 2 0
―――

15 H T U
  4 3 6
+ 1 1 8
―――

16 H T U
  4 3 6
+ 1 1 6
―――

Let's investigate

Make up two more sums to give a number pattern.

H T U
3 4 2
+ 1 0 2
―――

B Copy the squares, and finish them.
Find the magic numbers.

1

6	11	4
	7	
10		

2

12	7	
5		13
10	11	

3 Add 1 to every number.
Is it a magic square?

4	9	2
3	5	7
8	1	6

4 Add 10 to every number.
Is it a magic square?

Copy the crosses.
Complete them to make magic numbers.
Use the numbers 2, 4, 6, 7, 8 each time.

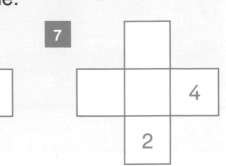

5

4	7	
	8	

6

	6	
2	7	

7

		4
	2	

8
27 + 38 = 65
26 + 39 = 65
25 + 40 = 65
24 + □ = 65
□ + □ = 65
□ + □ = 65
□ + □ = 65
□ + □ = 65

9
20 + 26 = 46
18 + 28 = 46
16 + □ = 46
□ + 32 = 46
□ + □ = 46
□ + □ = 46
□ + □ = 46
□ + □ = 46

10 Add the scores.

Emma

First game   236
Second game 418

Harry

First game   304
Second game 378

11 Who scored the most?

37

Let's investigate

Add 3s and 5s.
Try to make all the numbers up to 20.

Are there numbers you
can't make?
What are they?

C   Copy this puzzle. Solve the clues.

Down

1. Four hundred and eighteen
add one hundred and forty-three.

2. Add five hundred and fifty-four
to three hundred and nine.

5. Double forty-six.

Across

1. 309 + 219   **3.** 39 + 29   **4.** 87 + 106

Let's investigate

Make up clues for this cross-number puzzle.

Across	Down
1.	**1.**
3.	**2.**

38

Number 12

A

1	2	3	4	5	6	7	8	9	10
11	12	13	14	15	16	17	18	19	20
21	22	23	24	25	26	27	28	29	30
31	32	33	34	35	36	37	38	39	40
41	42	43	44	45	46	47	48	49	50
51	52	53	54	55	56	57	58	59	60
61	62	63	64	65	66	67	68	69	70
71	72	73	74	75	76	77	78	79	80
81	82	83	84	85	86	87	88	89	90
91	92	93	94	95	96	97	98	99	100

Use a 100 number square.

Colour these patterns.

1 Start on 95. Count back in 10s. End on 5.

2 Start on 93. Count back in 10s. End on 3.

3 Start on 99. Count back in 10s. End on 9.

4 Start on 97. Count back in 10s. End on 7.

Do these. Use the 100 square.

5
13 − 5
23 − 5
33 − 5
43 − 5
53 − 5
63 − 5
73 − 5
83 − 5
93 − 5

6
14 − 9
24 − 9
34 − 9
44 − 9
54 − 9
64 − 9
74 − 9
84 − 9
94 − 9

7
16 − 8
26 − 8
36 − 8
46 − 8
56 − 8
66 − 8
76 − 8
86 − 8
96 − 8

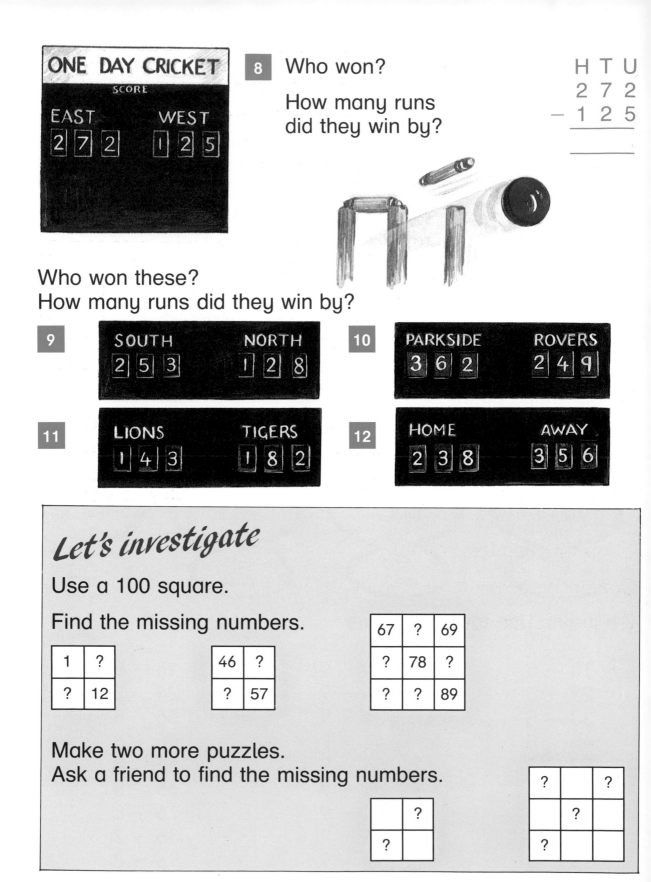

ONE DAY CRICKET
SCORE

EAST	WEST
2 7 2	1 2 5

8 Who won?

How many runs did they win by?

```
H T U
2 7 2
- 1 2 5
─────
```

Who won these?
How many runs did they win by?

9

SOUTH	NORTH
2 5 3	1 2 8

10

PARKSIDE	ROVERS
3 6 2	2 4 9

11

LIONS	TIGERS
1 4 3	1 8 2

12

HOME	AWAY
2 3 8	3 5 6

Let's investigate

Use a 100 square.

Find the missing numbers.

1	?
?	12

46	?
?	57

67	?	69
?	78	?
?	?	89

Make two more puzzles.
Ask a friend to find the missing numbers.

	?
?	

?		?
	?	
?		

B

	1	2	3	4	5	6	7	8	9	10
										20
				24						30
				34						40
										50
										60
										70
							77			80
		83								90
										100

1 Copy this.

Write the numbers that make the thing.

Look for number patterns.

2
131 − 16
141 − 16
151 − 16
161 − 16

3
247 − 19
347 − 19
447 − 19
547 − 19

4
356 − 137
456 − 137
556 − 137
656 − 137

Copy this number square.

Colour the answers to the subtractions.

What letter do you get?

215	416	27
237	228	314
229	29	316

5
```
H T U
4 9 1
- 2 6 3
```

6
```
H T U
5 6 1
- 5 3 4
```

7
```
H T U
4 3 4
- 2 1 9
```

8
```
H T U
7 4 3
- 4 2 7
```

9
```
H T U
3 7 0
- 1 3 3
```

10
```
H T U
9 4 2
- 6 2 8
```

11
```
H T U
4 3 6
- 2 0 7
```

Let's investigate

Make up different subtractions.
They must each have an answer of 124.

C John wanted 325 stickers. He made this chart.

1 John collected 50 stickers during week 1.
How many did he collect during week 2?

107 − 50 = ☐

2 How many did he collect during week 3?

3 How many more did he get during week 4?

4 How many did he collect during week 5?

5 How many does he still need?

6 Do you think John will collect all 325
stickers by the end of week 6? Why?

	325 stickers
Week 5	280
Week 4	225
Week 3	175
Week 2	107
Week 1	50

Let's investigate

Use the numbers 1 to 100.

Make two different 100 squares.
Start like this each time.

1	2	3	4	5	6	7	8	9	10
									11

Colour different patterns on each 100 square.
For example, 2   4   6   8 . . .

Shape 3

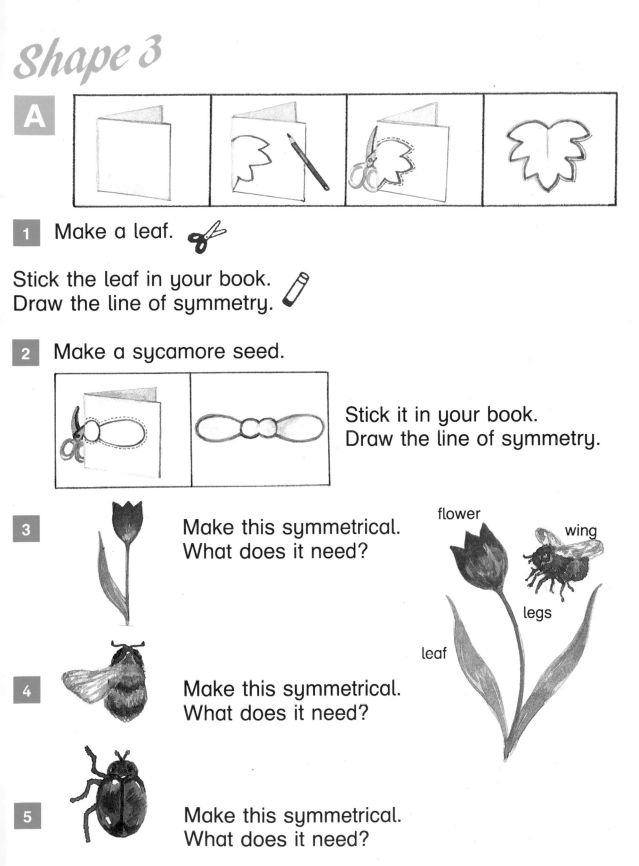

1 Make a leaf.

Stick the leaf in your book.
Draw the line of symmetry.

2 Make a sycamore seed.

Stick it in your book.
Draw the line of symmetry.

flower

wing

legs

leaf

3 Make this symmetrical.
What does it need?

4 Make this symmetrical.
What does it need?

5 Make this symmetrical.
What does it need?

Let's investigate

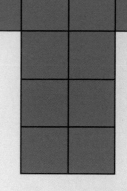

This shape has symmetry.

Draw more shapes with symmetry.
Use 12 squares each time.

B **1** Look carefully at this picture.

Fold a piece of paper in half.
Draw and cut out the butterfly.

Colour it.

Draw the line of symmetry.

2 Make two more butterflies.

3 Make a cut-out elephant.
Use a piece of folded paper.

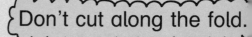
Don't cut along the fold.

Colour the elephant.
Stand it up.

Copy these shapes.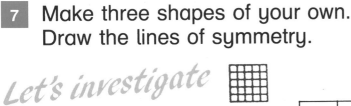
Use your ruler to draw the line of symmetry.

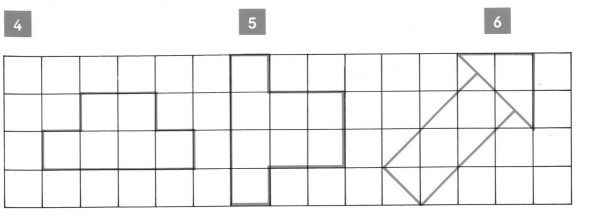

7 Make three shapes of your own.
Draw the lines of symmetry.

Let's investigate

Copy this pattern.

Colour the left side
to give symmetry.

Make another pattern
with symmetry.

C *Let's investigate*

Make two shapes like this.

Use them to make
a symmetrical shape.

Draw the shape. Put on the line of symmetry.

Make other symmetrical shapes.

Number 13

A How many pieces of chocolate are there?

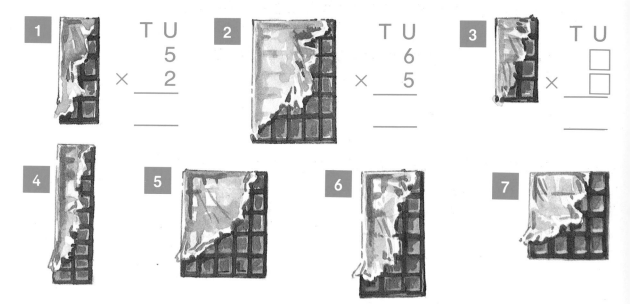

1.
$$
\begin{array}{r}
\text{T U} \\
5 \\
\times \quad 2 \\
\hline
\end{array}
$$

2.
$$
\begin{array}{r}
\text{T U} \\
6 \\
\times \quad 5 \\
\hline
\end{array}
$$

3.
$$
\begin{array}{r}
\text{T U} \\
\square \\
\times \quad \square \\
\hline
\end{array}
$$

Let's investigate

Find ways of putting
12 squares into bars.
Draw the different ways.

B

1. How many pieces are in 5 bars of KitKat?

2. How many pieces are in 8 bars of KitKat?

3. How many Milky Way bars in 4 packets?

4. How many Milky Way bars in 7 packets?

Find the word. Each answer gives you a letter.

5	T U
	6
×	2
	——

6	T U
	9
×	4
	——

7	T U
	8
×	3
	——

8	T U
	4
×	3
	——

9	T U
	6
×	4
	——

10	T U
	7
×	5
	——

11	T U
	7
×	3
	——

12	T U
	9
×	3
	——

13	T U
	8
×	2
	——

What is the word?

a	c	e	h	l	o	t
21	12	16	36	35	24	27

Let's investigate

Here are three numbers.

Add the two outside numbers.
Double the middle number.
What do you notice?

Find other sets of three numbers that do this.

C   Find these numbers.

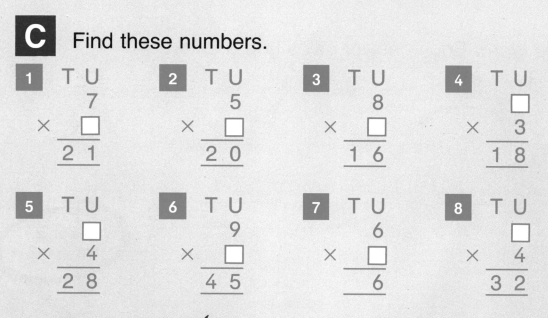

1 T U
         7
  × □
  ‾‾‾‾‾
  2 1

2 T U
         5
  × □
  ‾‾‾‾‾
  2 0

3 T U
         8
  × □
  ‾‾‾‾‾
  1 6

4 T U
         □
  × 3
  ‾‾‾‾‾
  1 8

5 T U
         □
  × 4
  ‾‾‾‾‾
  2 8

6 T U
         9
  × □
  ‾‾‾‾‾
  4 5

7 T U
         6
  × □
  ‾‾‾‾‾
    6

8 T U
         □
  × 4
  ‾‾‾‾‾
  3 2

Let's investigate

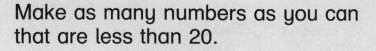

Make as many numbers as you can
that are less than 20.

You may use the × sign and each number
as many times as you like.

Area 3

A Write the area of these shapes.

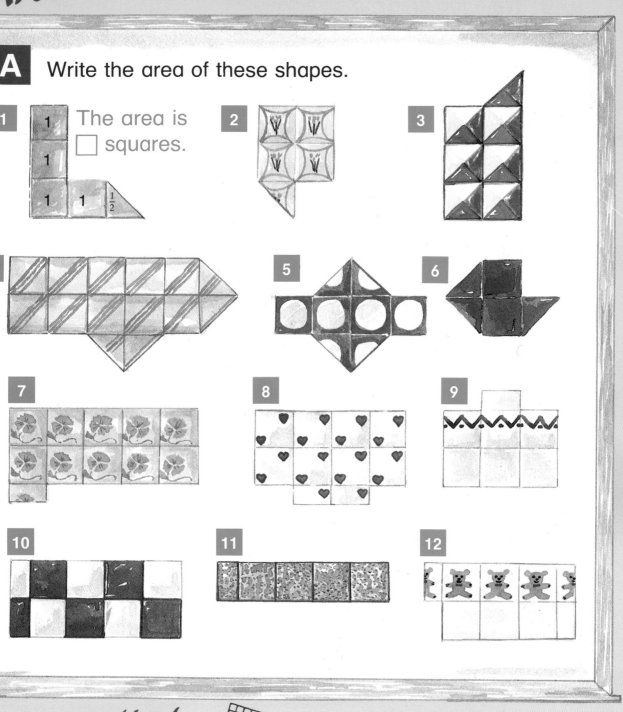

1
| 1 |
| 1 |
| 1 | 1 | $\frac{1}{2}$ |

The area is ☐ squares.

2

3

4

5

6

7

8

9

10

11

12

Let's investigate

Draw different shapes with an area of $12\frac{1}{2}$ squares.
Colour them.

49

The area is ☐ squares.

1

2

3

4

5

6

Let's investigate

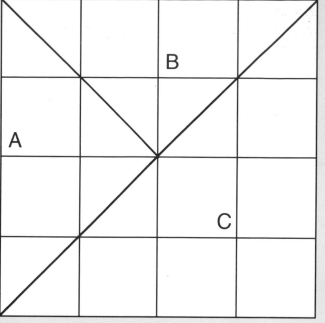

Draw these triangles.
Label them A, B and C.
Cut them out.

Write the area of
each triangle.

Make a rectangle using
all three triangles.

Draw it and write its area.

Now use two triangles to make
a square and then a larger triangle.

Draw the shapes you make. Write their areas.

C

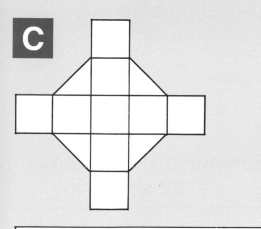

1 Here is a pattern.
What is its area?

2 Draw your own pattern.
Use some half squares.

Write the area
of your pattern.

Let's investigate

Draw a triangle whose area is $\frac{1}{2}$ square.

Draw two more triangles whose areas are
1 square and 2 squares.

Draw some more triangles. Write the area of each.

Number 14

A

1 How many shoes are in 14 shoe-bags?

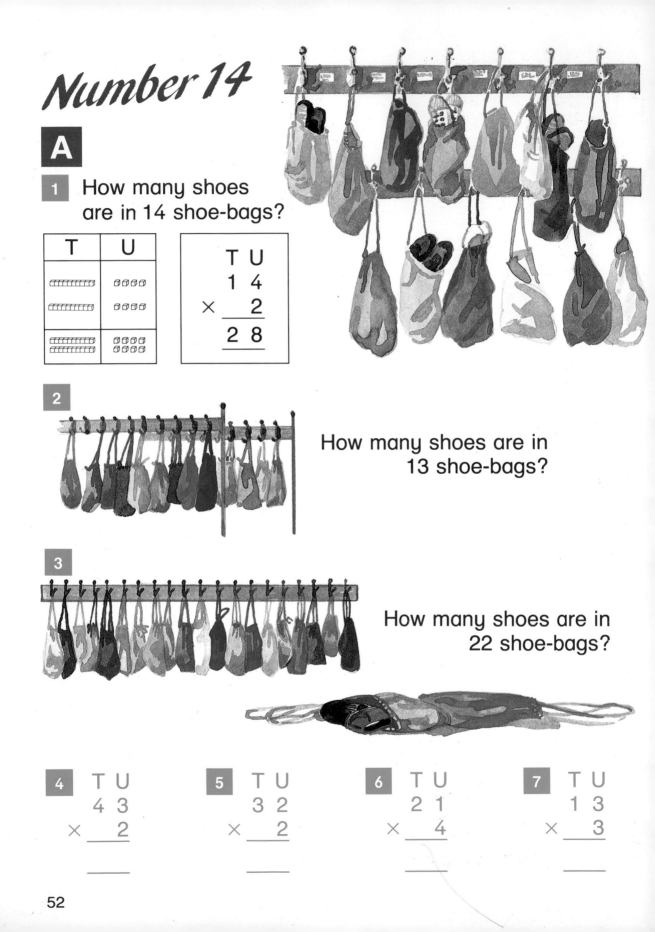

T	U
⫘⫘	🩰🩰🩰🩰
⫘⫘	🩰🩰🩰🩰
⫘⫘	🩰🩰🩰🩰 🩰🩰🩰🩰

```
  T U
  1 4
×   2
─────
  2 8
```

2 How many shoes are in 13 shoe-bags?

3 How many shoes are in 22 shoe-bags?

4
```
  T U
  4 3
×   2
─────
```

5
```
  T U
  3 2
×   2
─────
```

6
```
  T U
  2 1
×   4
─────
```

7
```
  T U
  1 3
×   3
─────
```

8 19 children dance.

How many feet
are there?

9 16 children have PE.

How many feet
are there?

10
```
T U
2 7
× 2
___
```

11
```
T U
2 5
× 2
___
```

12
```
T U
4 5
× 2
___
```

13
```
T U
1 7
× 3
___
```

14
```
T U
3 8
× 2
___
```

15
```
T U
2 6
× 3
___
```

16
```
T U
1 4
× 5
___
```

17
```
T U
2 3
× 4
___
```

18 29 × 3   **19** 17 × 4   **20** 19 × 5

Let's investigate

Put these numbers in pairs.

Each pair must give the same answer
when you multiply them.

This school has 4 classes.
There are 24 children
in each class.

1 How many children are in 3 classes?

2 How many children are in the school?

3 25×3

4 47×2

5 15×3

6 26×2

7 13×5

8 18×4

9

×	2	5
15		
18		90

10

×	16	19
3		
4		

Let's investigate

Find pairs of numbers to make 48,
like this. ☐ × ☐ = 48.

C

The children in Class 4 are in groups of 3.

Each child needs
2 paintbrushes,
3 pieces of paper
and 5 crayons.

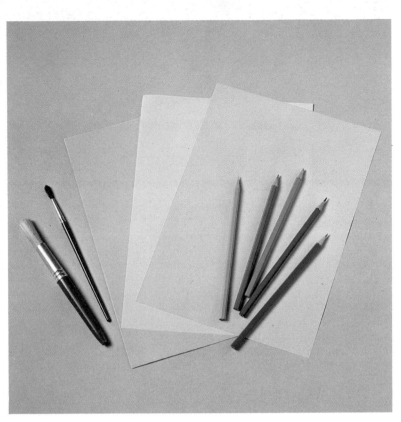

1   How many paintbrushes for 3 groups?

2   How many pieces of paper for 5 groups?

3   How many crayons for 6 groups?

Let's investigate

Use three different numbers.
Multiply them together.
The answer must be less than 25.

What sets of numbers can you find?

Data 3

A

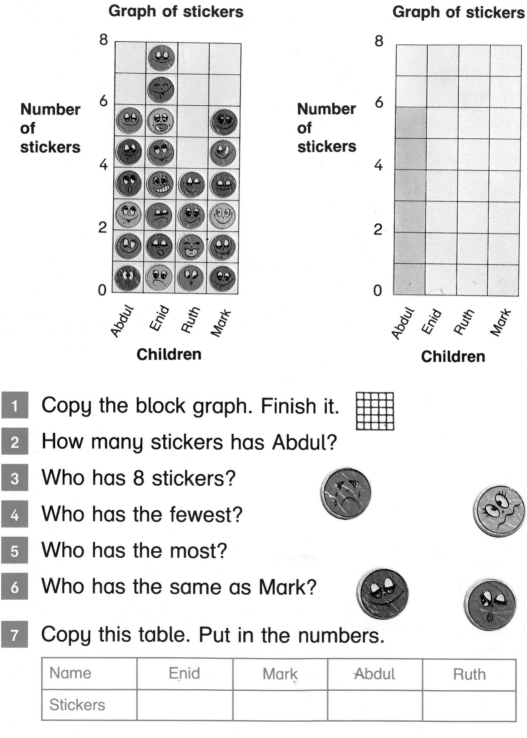

Graph of stickers

Number of stickers

Children

Graph of stickers

Number of stickers

Children

1 Copy the block graph. Finish it.

2 How many stickers has Abdul?

3 Who has 8 stickers?

4 Who has the fewest?

5 Who has the most?

6 Who has the same as Mark?

7 Copy this table. Put in the numbers.

Name	Enid	Mark	Abdul	Ruth
Stickers				

56

The children collect badges.

Enid has 12 badges.
Ruth has 16.
Mark has 18.
Abdul has 15.

8 Draw a block graph.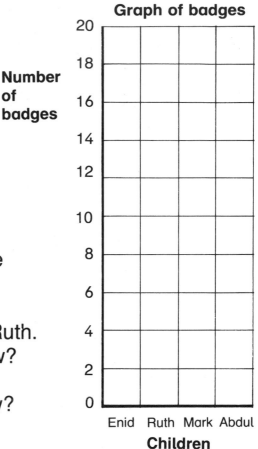

9 Who has the most badges?

10 How many do the children have altogether?

11 Enid gives 6 of her badges to Ruth. How many does Ruth have now?

12 How many does Enid have now?

Graph of badges

Number of badges

Children: Enid Ruth Mark Abdul

Let's investigate

Copy the graph.

Write a title and labels.

Write some questions about the graph.

Draw a table for it.

?				
?				

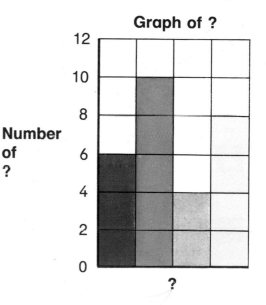

Graph of ?

Number of ?

?

B

Some children collect rubbers.

Susan has 16.
Marie has 22.
Alec has 13.
Brian has 20.
Angela has 18.

1. Draw a block graph.
   Write the title and labels.

2. Who has most rubbers?

3. How many more has
   Angela than Alec?

4. How many fewer has Alec
   than Brian?

5. Who do you think has
   collected rubbers for the
   longest time?

6. Who has the fewest?
   Why do you think this is?

7. How many do the girls
   have altogether?

8. Draw a table for the graph.

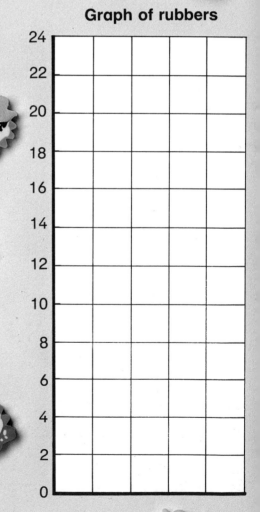

Graph of rubbers

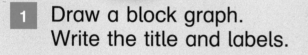

Let's investigate

Leroy collects stamps.

Canada 24	France 30	USA 40	Spain 15

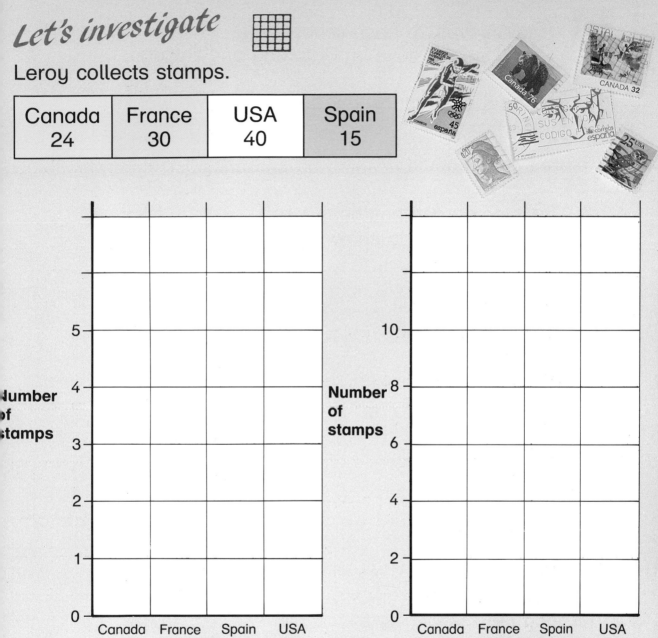

Which graph would you show Leroy's stamps on?
Why did you choose it?

Draw the graph.
Write the title and labels.

Write some questions about the graph.

59

C Paula saves 2p each school day.
She does not save on Saturday and Sunday.

1 Draw a table to show her savings for two weeks.

M	T	W	Th	F	Sa	Su	M	T	W	Th	F	Sa	Su
2p	4p												

2 This block graph has been torn.
Draw a new one to show Paula's savings.

Let's investigate

Draw these graphs.

Put on numbers so that they both show the same number of soaps.

60

Money 3

$122p = £1·22$

100 pennies make £1. 100p = £1·00

1	$115p = £\boxed{·}$	2	$127p = £\boxed{·}$
3	$136p = £\boxed{·}$	4	$142p = £\boxed{·}$
5	$105p = £\boxed{·}$	6	$108p = £\boxed{·}$
7	$64p = £\boxed{·}$	8	$82p = £\boxed{·}$

How much money is in these bank books?

9

	£	
	2	36
+	4	12
Total		

10

	£	
	3	47
+	1	17
Total		

11

	£	
	4	47
+	3	31
Total		

12

	£	
	5	28
+	2	62
Total		

13

	£	
	6	37
+	3	57
Total		

14

	£	
	7	78
+	1	15
Total		

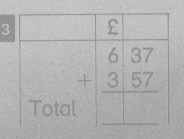

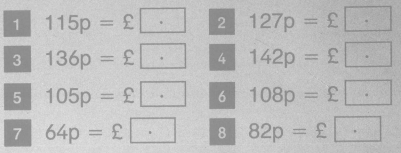

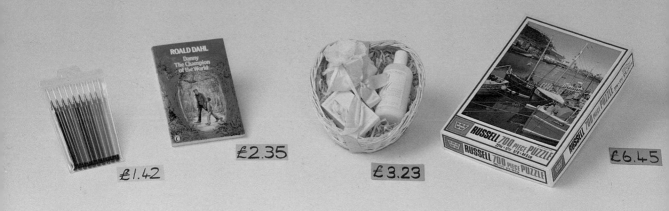

£2.35 £1.42 £3.23 £6.45

15

	£
Lisa has	2 · 64
She spends	1 · 42
She has	_____ left

16

	£
Tom has	4 · 58
He spends	2 · 35
He has	_____ left

17

	£
Fay has	5 · 79
She spends	3 · 23
She has	_____ left

18

	£
Simon has	7 · 67
He spends	6 · 45
He has	_____ left

Let's investigate

Put coins in each pot.
The money in the pots must add up to £1·60.

+   +   =   £1·60

Find different ways.

B

Add up the savings.

1 Darren

£	
2	24
+ 4	38

2 Ela

£	
3	55
+ 3	38

3 Rupa

£	
2	06
+ 5	77

4 Luke

£	
6	38
+ 1	46

5 Emma

£	
3	59
+ 4	29

6 Cheryl

£	
3	77
+ 3	15

7 Who has the least money?

8 Who has the most money?

9 Darren saved another £1·29. How much does he have?

10 Emma took out £4·27. How much is left?

11 Cheryl took out £2·52. How much is left?

12 Luke took out £6·33. How much is left?

13	pence	124p	136p	150p		37p		101p		
	£	£1·24			£1·17		£0·63		£1·09	£1·70

Let's investigate

What are the missing numbers?

Do the same sum again.
Use different numbers.

Find more ways.

$$\begin{array}{r} £ \\ 4 \cdot 4\ 7 \\ +\ 1 \cdot \square\ 6 \\ \hline 5 \cdot \square\ 3 \end{array}$$

C

1 You have £1·50 in the bank.
You save £1·25 each week.
How much will you have after 2 weeks?

2 How much will you have after 5 weeks?

3 How much will you have after 10 weeks?

Let's investigate

You have £2·00.

Choose three parcels
to buy.

You must have
only 1p left.

35p
41p
44p
52p
80p
78p
64p

64

Number 15

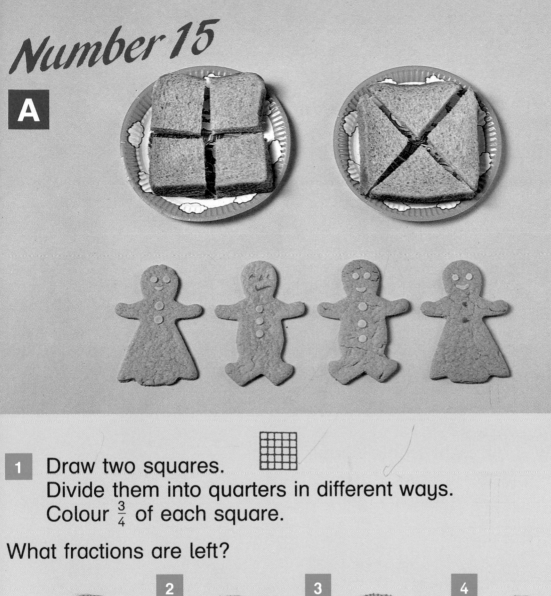

1 Draw two squares.
Divide them into quarters in different ways.
Colour $\frac{3}{4}$ of each square.

What fractions are left?

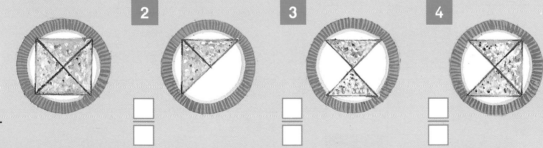

$\frac{4}{4}$ **2** ☐/☐   **3** ☐/☐   **4** ☐/☐

5 What fraction of the gingerbread people have eyes?

6 What fraction have buttons?

7 What fraction have eyes and buttons?

8 Draw four buns.
Colour $\frac{3}{4}$ of them.

9 Draw four biscuits.
Colour $\frac{1}{4}$ of them.

What fraction is not coloured?

Let's investigate

This is $\frac{1}{4}$ of a shape.
Draw the whole shape.

Use ▢▢ again.

Draw a different whole shape.

B **1** Copy the puzzle. Solve the clues.

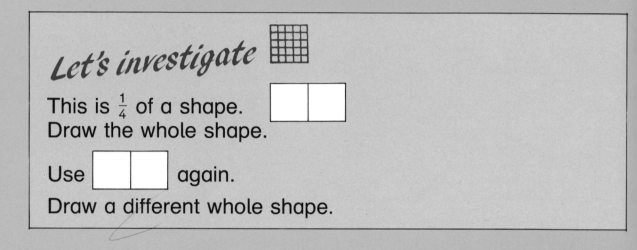

Across

1. $\frac{1}{2}$ of ▢ = 6

3. $\frac{1}{2}$ of 20 = ▢

4. $\frac{1}{4}$ of 12 = ▢

5. $\frac{1}{2}$ of 12 = ▢

6. $\frac{1}{2}$ of 18 = ▢

7. $\frac{1}{2}$ of 10 = ▢

Down

2. 5 is $\frac{1}{4}$ of ▢

3. 8 is $\frac{1}{2}$ of ▢

2 Draw this shape.
Colour $\frac{3}{4}$ of it.

$\frac{1}{4}$ of ☐ squares = ☐ squares

$\frac{3}{4}$ of ☐ squares = ☐ squares

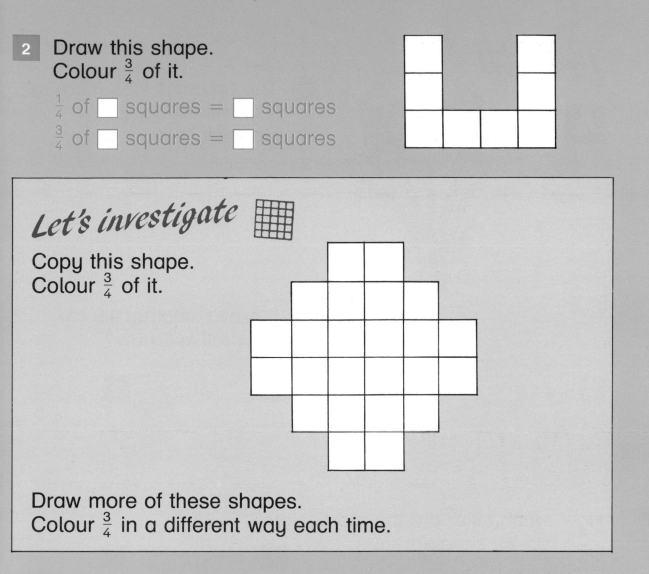

Let's investigate

Copy this shape.
Colour $\frac{3}{4}$ of it.

Draw more of these shapes.
Colour $\frac{3}{4}$ in a different way each time.

C *Let's investigate*

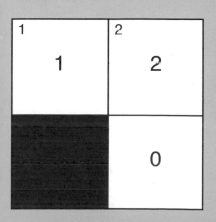

Make up some clues.

Across

1. $\frac{\square}{\square}$ of ☐

Down

2. $\frac{\square}{\square}$ of ☐

Make another puzzle yourself.

Length 3

A

1 The amarylis was 8 cm tall.
It grows 13 cm.
How tall is it?

```
    cm
     8
 + 1 3
 ─────
```

2 It grows another 15 cm.
How tall is it now?

3
```
    cm
   1 5
 +   9
 ─────
```

4
```
    cm
   2 7
 + 1 6
 ─────
```

5
```
    cm
   3 7
 + 1 8
 ─────
```

6
```
    cm
   4 6
 + 2 4
 ─────
```

How much taller are the red flowers?

7

13 cm 18 cm

8

21 cm 26 cm

9

5 cm 16 cm

10

12 cm 17 cm

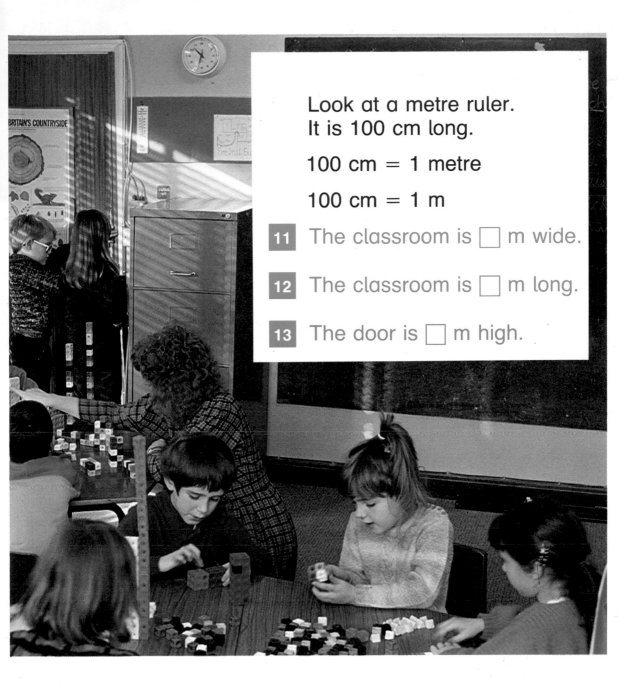

Look at a metre ruler.
It is 100 cm long.

100 cm = 1 metre

100 cm = 1 m

11 The classroom is ☐ m wide.

12 The classroom is ☐ m long.

13 The door is ☐ m high.

Let's investigate

What can you buy about 1 metre long?

What can you buy more than 5 metres long?

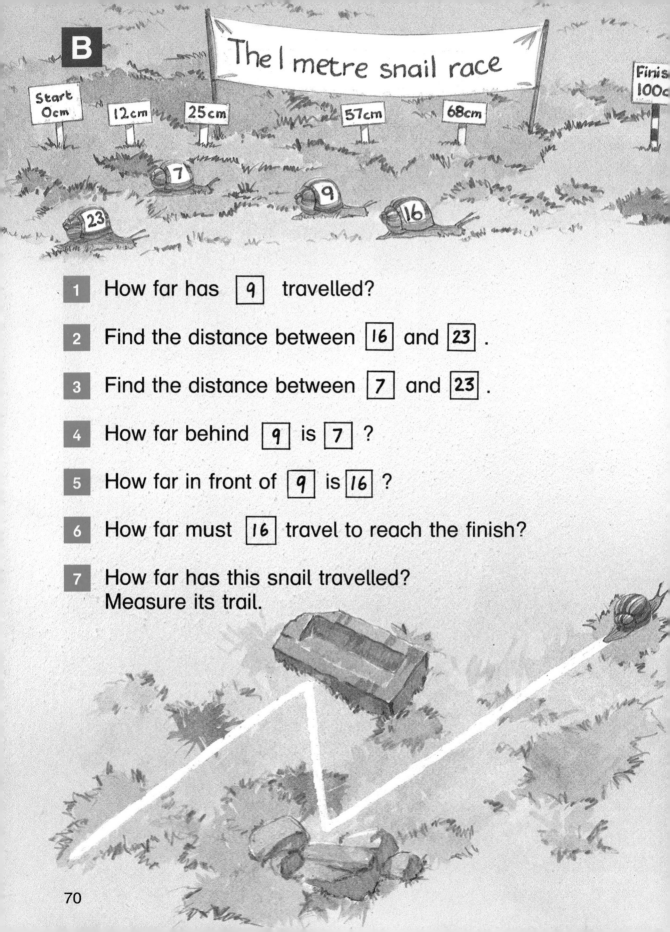

B The 1 metre snail race

Start 0cm | 12cm | 25cm | 57cm | 68cm | Finis 100c

1. How far has ⑨ travelled?

2. Find the distance between ⑯ and ㉓.

3. Find the distance between ⑦ and ㉓.

4. How far behind ⑨ is ⑦?

5. How far in front of ⑨ is ⑯?

6. How far must ⑯ travel to reach the finish?

7. How far has this snail travelled?
   Measure its trail.

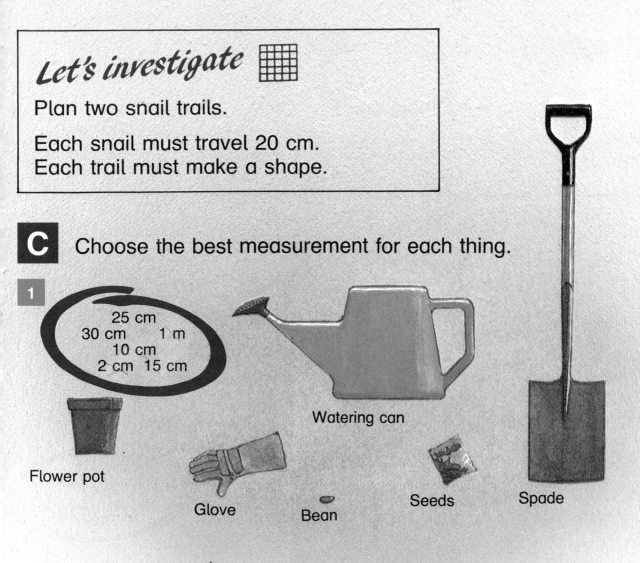

Let's investigate

Plan two snail trails.

Each snail must travel 20 cm.
Each trail must make a shape.

C   Choose the best measurement for each thing.

1

25 cm
30 cm   1 m
10 cm
2 cm   15 cm

Watering can

Flower pot

Glove

Bean

Seeds

Spade

Let's investigate

What am I ?   I am 2m long
I am made from wood
I have shelves
I have books on me

Choose something in the classroom and measure it.

Write some clues for a friend to guess what it is.
Start with the measurement.

Do some more.

Weight 3

1000 g is 1 kilogram.

A

1 Find something that weighs about 1 kg.
Check the weight.

1 kg means 1 kilogram.

2 Get a plastic bag.
Put books in it to weigh 1 kg.

Write the names of the books.

3 Write ways to balance 1 kg.

1 kg = 500 g + ☐ g
1 kg = 200 g + 200 g + ☐ g + ☐ g

4 Heavy things are weighed in kilograms.

*5 kg 6000 kg
3000 kg
700 kg 25 kg
90 kg*

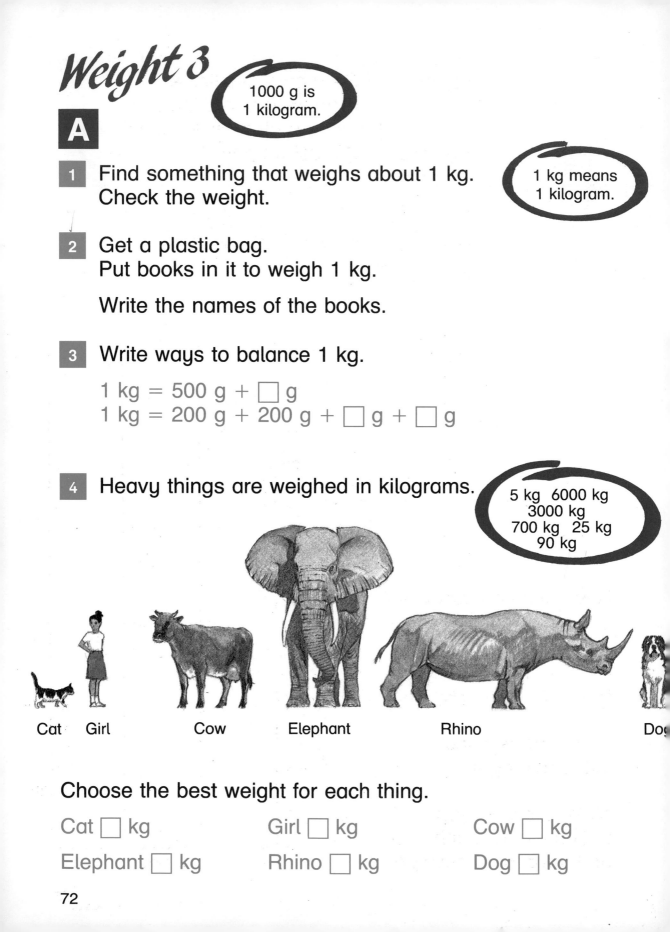

Cat   Girl   Cow   Elephant   Rhino   Dog

Choose the best weight for each thing.

Cat ☐ kg   Girl ☐ kg   Cow ☐ kg

Elephant ☐ kg   Rhino ☐ kg   Dog ☐ kg

72

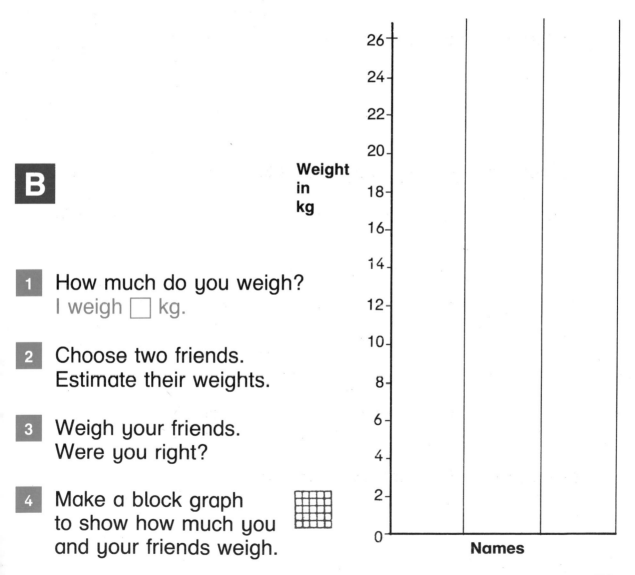

Let's investigate

$\frac{1}{2}$ kg = 500 g

Get some plasticine.
Work with some friends.
Make a plasticine animal.
It must weigh $\frac{1}{2}$ kg.

B

1 How much do you weigh?
I weigh ☐ kg.

2 Choose two friends.
Estimate their weights.

3 Weigh your friends.
Were you right?

4 Make a block graph
to show how much you
and your friends weigh.

Weight
in
kg

26
24
22
20
18
16
14
12
10
8
6
4
2
0

Names

Cat 5 kg

St Bernard
dog
90 kg

C

1 How much do you weigh?
Estimate how many cats
together weigh the same as you.

2 Estimate how many children of about
your weight weigh the same as the dog.

3 Estimate how many children would
weigh the same as the cow.

4 Estimate how many cows would
weigh the same as the elephant.

Cow
700 kg

Let's investigate

Estimate the total weight
of your class.
How did you do it?

How many classes like yours
would weigh about the same
as an elephant?

Elephant
6000 kg

Time 3

Big Ben is the famous clock tower that stands beside the Houses of Parliament in London.
Big Ben is really the name of the bell that strikes the hour.

A Write the times.

o'clock
half past
quarter past

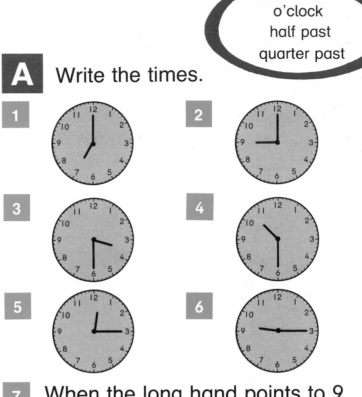

1

2

3

4

5

6

7 When the long hand points to 9, it is quarter to something.

A clock shows quarter to 12. Draw the clock.

Write the times.

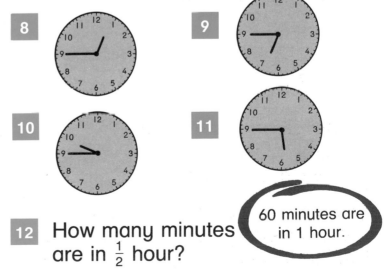

8

9

10

11

12 How many minutes are in $\frac{1}{2}$ hour?

60 minutes are in 1 hour.

75

13 These clocks show
9 hours 30 minutes.

Draw the clocks.

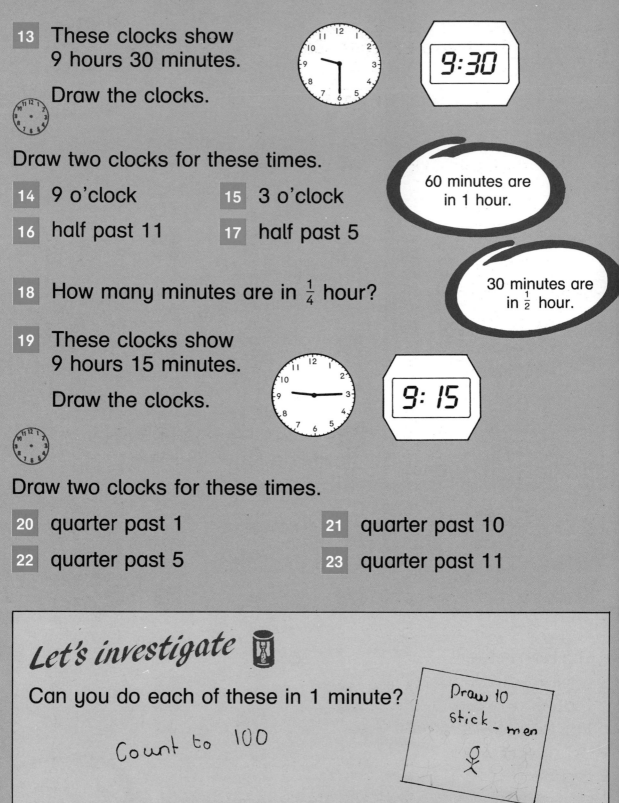

Draw two clocks for these times.

14 9 o'clock

15 3 o'clock

16 half past 11

17 half past 5

> 60 minutes are in 1 hour.

18 How many minutes are in $\frac{1}{4}$ hour?

> 30 minutes are in $\frac{1}{2}$ hour.

19 These clocks show
9 hours 15 minutes.

Draw the clocks.

Draw two clocks for these times.

20 quarter past 1

21 quarter past 10

22 quarter past 5

23 quarter past 11

Let's investigate

Can you do each of these in 1 minute?

Count to 100

Draw 10 stick-men

Write other things that take about 1 minute.

B

1 Put these in order. Start with the earliest time.

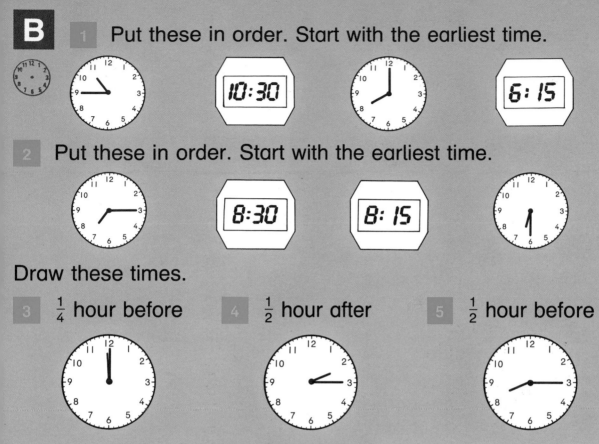

2 Put these in order. Start with the earliest time.

Draw these times.

3 $\frac{1}{4}$ hour before   **4** $\frac{1}{2}$ hour after   **5** $\frac{1}{2}$ hour before

Let's investigate

Write things that happen in school.

What takes about $\frac{1}{4}$ hour?

What takes about $\frac{1}{2}$ hour?

What takes about 1 hour?

C Let's investigate

You need some times of television programmes.

Find programmes that last 15 minutes.

Find programmes that last $\frac{1}{2}$ hour.

Find programmes that last longer than $\frac{1}{2}$ hour.

Angles 3

A

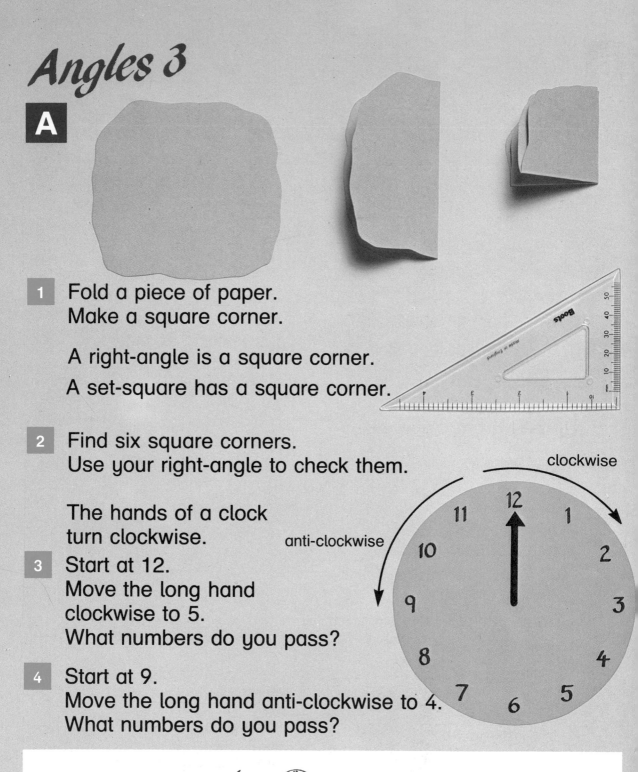

1. Fold a piece of paper.
   Make a square corner.

   A right-angle is a square corner.

   A set-square has a square corner.

2. Find six square corners.
   Use your right-angle to check them.

   clockwise

   The hands of a clock
   turn clockwise.

   anti-clockwise

3. Start at 12.
   Move the long hand
   clockwise to 5.
   What numbers do you pass?

4. Start at 9.
   Move the long hand anti-clockwise to 4.
   What numbers do you pass?

Let's investigate

Draw some times with right-angles between the hands.

Make a clock like this one.

1 Point the hand to 12.
Move it clockwise one
right angle.
Where does it point now?

2 Point the hand to 12.
Move it clockwise
two right angles.
Where does it point now?

3 Point the hand to 2.
Move it clockwise
one right angle.
Where does it point now?

4 Find the right angles
in this pattern.
How many are there?

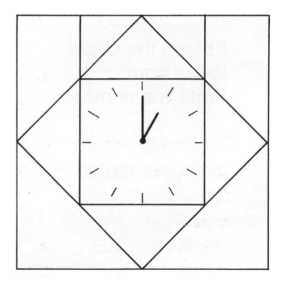

Let's investigate

Draw shapes with right-angles.
This shape has two right angles.
Draw shapes with 2, 3, 4, 5 and
6 right angles.

C

1 Make a dial.
Use these things.

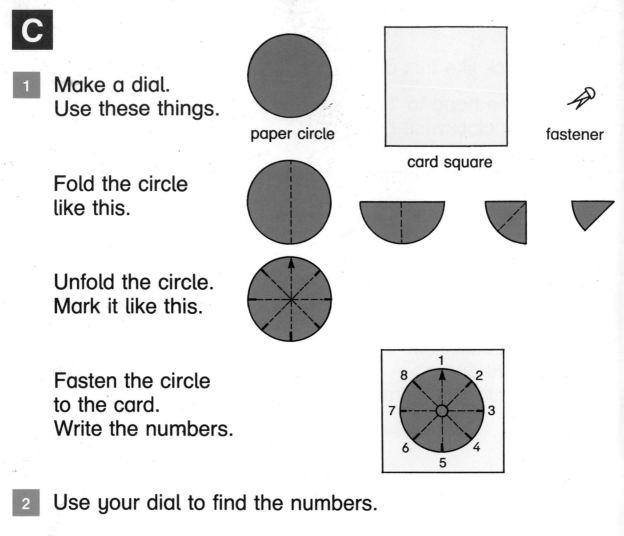

paper circle

card square

fastener

Fold the circle
like this.

Unfold the circle.
Mark it like this.

Fasten the circle
to the card.
Write the numbers.

2 Use your dial to find the numbers.

Point the ↑ to 1
Turn clockwise one right - angle
Turn anti - clockwise two right - angles
Turn clock wise three right angles.
The number is 1 ☐ ☐ ☐

Let's investigate

Make up some different numbers.
Write the instructions.
Let your friend find the numbers.